This-Ability: How my Learning dis-Ability became my way to Financial Freedom

By Matthew T. Sampson Jr.

First Edition: April 2023

This-Ability: How my Learning dis-Ability became my way to Financial Freedom /By Matthew T. Sampson Jr.

ISBN: 978-1-943616-54-1

Publisher: MAWMedia Group, LLC
Los Angeles | Reno | Nashville

DEDICATION PAGE

I dedicate this book to my mother Lois, grandmother Juanita, and grandfather Robert Sr.; my elementary school Special Education teacher, Lorilie Mitchelle at Paden School in Vacaville California; and my real estate mentor, Luis Castillo Munoz.

You each believed in me and molded me into the productive adult I am today.

ACKNOWLEDGEMENT

To my Mother Lois and my father Matthew Sr.: Both of my parents always showed me love, propelling me towards all my achievements. They always supported me in the best way they knew possible. My grandmother Juanita was always there. She would listen to me when I cried to her about school. She would give advice. She would comfort me before bed. My grandfather Robert Sr. gave strength and taught me how to explore places... to the hardware store, evening walks to look at homes being built. He would tell me his landlord stories. He taught me how to be hands on DIY and to be fearless in the face of good risks. I also thank my sister Aubin for being patient with me with encouragement. She never gave me any trouble during the year I was in school about my learning deficit. She gave me my space. My other sister Pearl-Fatime always encouraged me towards my goals also in my 20s & 30s. She always acknowledged me for setting a good example for her.

I would like to also acknowledge the educators who positively impacted me and believed in me. I would like to start off with my preschool teacher, Mrs. Eddie. I remember her being patient with me. She would always have a smile on her face. She always told me I was smart. My 2nd and 3rd grade teacher, Deidre Seibert; my 4th, 5th, and 6th grade teacher, Lorelei Mitchell. All were awesome teachers. They made learning fun. They always had learning games for the students. They came out of pocket. They were genuine. I remember them as understanding and nurturing in their strategy handling my learning deficit. In Jr. High School, Judy Fanning and Kathy Uline were effective educators, supportive fun, positive and supportive. Kelley Crismon, my history teacher, encouraged me to read in front of a class. She showed me not to be afraid to read out loud. Teacher's Assistants Gina Urewicz, Cynthia McGowan, and Linda Harstgrove were always supportive. I appreciated their help. They always encouraged and supported me.

I would like to thank my friends I have known from elementary into adulthood for supporting me throughout my journey: Jay Bariuan, Lilja Redwine, and Marisa J. Steier. High School appreciation goes to Lisa Nagle and the counselors who handed me my official diploma. I appreciate Mrs Greenwal and Mrs Allen. My other friends include Cristina Hudson, Christy Edwards, Jusin Hopper, Eva Arenas, and Stephanie Jones of Will C. Wood High School. Support through Solano College goes out to Department of Disability & Rehabilitation staff Arlene Cohen and counselor Sheryl. Thank you, Kristine Marie Gomez, Jaishea Crowford, Miesha, Ricky Lee, and Shavone. I appreciate my coworker Lindsay Mendez of Medical Records that hired me into my first position starting my hospital admininstrative career. She believed in me and accomodated my learning deficit with support from the Reginal Occupational Program of Solano County.

I appreciate the support from my colleagues over 15 years of my career in the Emergency Department. Robert Lara, Cristine Brazil, Angela Lara, Evangeline, Grace, and Jessica Potts. ED Tech Maria Fonseca, Cheryal Peacock, Angie P, and Antoinette known as Anne. Nurses: Regina Robinson, Kim Robinson, ANM Tiffany Petterson, and Manager Victoria Myers.

A BIG APPRECIATION goes out to Jennifer Chou for support throughout the process of this book.

Contents

Section I: Elementary Lessons

Chapter 1: Perfectly Normal Family

My grandfather passed away in 1997. I never considered that grief held a central role in my life. But, in my young life, I have buried my grandfather, my grandmother, my mother, and my mother's boyfriend. Grief is a trauma that exacts its toll slowly and subtly over time even after it has emphasized itself and demanded attention in the moment. The effect of multiple deaths of significant family members is compounded by a sense of powerlessness in the face of death. Years later, I can still cry at the mention or the mere thought of my mother's words, my grandfather's training patience, or my grandmother's helpful hands. Yet, grief was not the first lesson I learned about standing against powerlessness to find my way.

I learned woodworking from my grandfather among other things. He taught me about home repair with many DIY projects. He would always compare me to Trish, a neighbor girl. I think it was his old-school way of awakening my sense of competition. He hoped that something would turn on inside me to rise to my potential to excel in school. That would never be the case. Comparison has never worked to motivate me. Comparisons have always made me feel like I was less than the other persons. I have a learning disability that did not fit into the educational system at the time.

My grandfather was born in 1912 and did not finish secondary school. We never discussed it, but he had to have some type of disability. That may be why he did not finish school. It just didn't work for him either. He worked as a janitor his whole life. He and my grandmother did the lion share of raising my while my mother worked. I was kept in the house and did not go outside the home a lot. My mom was overprotective. But she worked a lot and left me with my grandparents.

My mother was vehemently opposed to me being a janitor. She was unreasonably preoccupied with the notion that this was all I was learning from my grandfather. She would say, "Don't you ever clean anyone's toilets." I am certain that she meant well.

My grandmother was a nurse, and in that capacity married below her educational status. I could always count on her to lament something like, "Robert doesn't have education or a job with benefits. I don't know why he does not want to do more." Her idea of success was confined to those two measurements. I am certain that they both meant well, but neither my mother nor my grandmother could see what my grandfather was: content. Neither of them seemed to comprehend that this contentment was the prize in life.

I wish I knew then what I know now. My grandfather was not just what he did as a job. He was more. In truth, we are all more than that. We are also more than our grades or what we achieve in school. If you can find contentment, you have found what millionaires go broke attempting to capture. If you can find contentment before your reach your retirement years, you have found what the richest people alive would trade their wealth for: time and contentment.

I followed in my grandfather's footsteps in property buying. Yes, he put his woodworking to work. Not only did he clean toilets in his day job, but he reworked bathrooms as well as kitchens, and bedrooms. He was more than a janitor. He was more than a property owner. He was greater than any disability. Even with the comparisons, he was my best friend while he was well. I can only hope to be as great a man as my grandfather was.

I learned from the ever-present example of both my grandparents. I was spoiled by them in a way. My grandmother was more of the anti-social type like a diner waitress who hated her job. She would often say smart comments and engage with a confrontational style as if attempting to push you away before you chose not to reject her. She had no friends and would not allow my grandpa to have his friends over.

My grandfather was more of a people person. He was less confrontational but, in tense situations, he was first to call names, punch below the belt, and attempt to hurt feelings. Neither of them was physically abusive nor corporal punishers. I remember my grandfather as he became ill and immobile. I took care of him during these years. He would grab my collar and threaten about what he could do if he wasn't disabled. But he nor my grandmother ever laid a hand on me. The hitting I got from my mother. She would hit with a flyswatter or slap me in the face.

Slapped

My mom would argue with teachers and take my side against them even as her patience for me at home dwindled. My mom had to come home after being stressed and attempt to teach me to read. She was an LVN nurse. She worked at a prison. She brought home the stress of engaging in such a rough environment. I remember her complaints about coworkers. Their actions meant that she would work a double shift or stay late at work. Her disagreements about assignments and disputes about her performance were a source of stress for her. She would always have more challenges with her coworkers than the inmates.

My mother and father were amid a split. That may have had something to do with her lack of patience and shallow threshold for disappointment. She and he were not on the same page. When he came to visit, they would argue. I had a sneaking suspicion then that their frustration with each other was a miscommunication of a deep-seated love for one another.

My mom would come to my room and invite me to read at the edge of the bed. Her lack of patience was quickly evident. It was okay in the beginning, but as I began to stumble on my words and sound them out, she would get frustrated. I remember learning about phonics, but the words I learned were only by memory. If I knew the word, it was because I had memorized it not because of an increase in my comprehension.

The teachers would provide sheets to work through phonics. I just saw them as combinations of letters, not words. I would try to remember prefixes and suffixes and put them together. They would not register. They did not go together in my mind to form anything discernable.

"Matthew! Try it out. Sound it out. Did you get it?" My mom would begin with cajoling steadily increasing her volume.

"No. I don't get it." I would get frustrated and pout. She would slap me for pouting. She would sometimes allow me to move to the next word. What she could not understand, I thought, was that it was easier for me to accept that she was frustrated and endure the slap than to read. I was not able to make it work. Sessions would end with me crying. The teacher would always require a signature for the homework. She would sign and that would be our required 20 minutes.

I felt worthless. I was stuck. No one knew how to help me. I would sleep in the same bed as my grandmother sometimes. I would tell her about how frustrated I was and the bad attitude I had. I became a behavior problem because I could not express my feelings. I felt like I was in a hole that I would not be able to dig myself out of. The pressures were about going to the next grade and staying current with my class. Everyone attempted to treat me with kindness, but I never felt it.

Later, I found that my mother had a disability as well. My father's side of the family experiences learning disabilities as well. I think that my mother felt that she did not want me to go through what she went through. She wanted me to be stronger. I found out through some relatives about the pervasive reading problems throughout my family.

More than Disability

I know that I am worth something. I know that people work within their power. Some don't know how to discover their power. I can redo an engine. I can fix most anything mechanical. Each of us must step out of our comfort zone and ask for help. Find a mentor that has overcome similar challenges and challenge yourself toward a clear goal. Accept that the process is baby steps. Move consistently at your own pace. Pick up the pace as you can. Refuse comparisons that make you feel slow. Use comparison to realize that you can achieve because others have achieved in their power.

When I learn in a situation of doing what I am learning, I learn faster. When I am under pressure with someone watching me, I have difficulty. I am great on life and practical situations. I can comprehend complex concepts like cryptocurrency and other constructs. I am good at the application of mathematical concepts. I am just not capable of articulating the process or the constructs. Find something that you are a natural in and you like. This is the perfect combination.

The messages you give kids make a difference. Though she would slap me, my mother told me, "Keep moving forward. They want you to give up. Never give that to them." Another thing my mom used to tell me was, "They want to see you fail!" Yet she was always high on education. I never knew who THEY were. "I am not always going to be here. Be persistent." That was her attitude. She did want me to allow THEM to make fun of me and discourage me. It is mainly because of her that I refused to make my learning disability a crutch.

Chapter 2: The Purpose of School

Level Playing Field

I did not know I was different. I was naïve. No one said anything. I did not know that what I was doing and experiencing was out of the norm. I had to work harder studying for hours just to get some of my math homework done. I was not interested. I faced and had to break through a brick wall with each assignment before I could proceed.

I was held back in kindergarten. I did not know that it was abnormal. You just attended two kindergarten classes. I was in one class in one school. Then, I was in that class again. It did not register until I was older and noticed that the other kids were ahead of me. I wanted to stay with my class once I noticed.

I acted out because I noticed that I was not keeping up. I had assistive devices that helped me to keep up. In school, I was always one of the last ones to finish. I was a class clown and was often rude or confrontational with other students.

18 This Ability

My grandpa used to call people stupid including me. It was a part of his vocabulary. I didn't necessarily take it personally. I would replicate that behavior in school. The kids would escalate the situation. I would further escalate and egg them on. I would end up in a fight with the kids. It was a frustration as well as a distraction from the schoolwork. My parents would tell me that if someone hit me, I should hit them back. I was probably rude and unruly.

It took until third grade for me to notice that something was different in the classes I was in. It was teachers that began to point out my smaller classes and comparisons to other teachers. It was in fourth grade that a teacher's assistant was frustrated and stated, "Other students are already past this. They already know this. You need to get on board."

"I'm trying." She made it seem like I was resisting on purpose. I began to act out because of my frustration with my ignorance and the lack of patience of the grown-ups around me.

I remember the teacher's assistant saying that I needed to know the information at this point in my academic career. It created anxiety for me. Even kids in the special education class were already reading. I realized that I was in a hole. The other kids could write and read faster than I could. I felt more made fun of by the teacher's assistant than the other students. I was the black sheep among the other learners.

If I could go back, I would educate that teacher's assistant to the fact that every learner is different. A blind person may not be able to see, but they are better at using their other senses than a person that relies on sight. I have the potential and strong ability in other things that the average person may not be able to do. I have a more intense because I did not have the reading to rely on.

I still have trouble with reading, but I can get by. The experience lowered my self-esteem as a child though I did not realize it. My confidence was lowered because I could not keep up with my classmates. My mother always told me to keep going even as she was hard on me. She did not want me to lose hope in myself. I would often be frustrated and cry.

Work Today: Remnants of Hesitation

Even today, I rang up a customer—the complexity of the job. I forgot to ring in a discount and provide samples. I felt the same feeling from when I was a child. Forgetting may be different, but I have the sense of worthlessness because my coworker remembered everything. I am more sensitive to comparisons as an adult. I don't feel worthlessness, but I do feel behind or that I should know this already.

I just transferred out of the emergency room after 15 years. It was hard for me to learn it. I transferred out and worked for optical sales. My trainers were getting frustrated. I could not keep up. She showed me all my mistakes. "We have a worker that was hired after you, but she has already picked up the job." I was crestfallen.

I felt like I was in elementary school again. I told her, "I have been going through this all my life. I like it here, but I need more time to learn it. The pressure is overwhelming."

I don't want to see accommodations as a crutch. I don't want to say that I can't do it. When I was hired, I often click that I do not have a disability. I don't want it to be an excuse for me not to get anywhere in life. I don't want to be like people that allow disability to be their reason for failing. But I spoke up and advocated for myself.

My manager started to give me more time, and employees changed their attitudes. They seemed to be more patient and allow me to get comfortable. Their lower agitation made room for my mental clarity. I was better able to pick up tasks, processes, and routines. I am doing better. I just needed more time to feel comfortable. I just needed support without comparisons to other people.

My Ability

I engaged some doctors and nurses who wanted to know about real estate. They describe the process just as I communicate it to them, but they are not able to put it into practice. They have the funds and the understanding, but they can't put it together. I have less and am able to process it and apply it. They have the same challenge I had with reading. They overcomplicate it.

I remember an older lady at my job that talked to me about the real estate I am into. A doctor turned around and looked at me like I had it made. I was shocked. I often think that if I did not have this learning difference, I could have a degree in medicine and be in the position she is in. Yet, I am in the same environment with them doing well in real estate while they don't see their opportunity to gain the freedom I have. At the same time, I see them with the brain power and the resources, but they see it in the opposite. I think it would be a breeze for them, but it is not. If it were, they would have done it already.

It is almost a curse for them that they were never challenged to see life or persevere in the way that I was forced to. I had to find a different way to understand and read, which translated into a brain that comprehends the complexity of mechanical repair, eBay, cryptocurrency, and real estate. I have embraced my learning difference because I had to. I wish others would open their minds and accept their creativity even when they are not forced into it. My mom was right. They want us to fail. Let's persevere with open minds, find our love, and express our power.

Chapter 3: Junior High

In junior high school, I began to go from one central class to mainstream classes changing classes with the other students. The only special education I had was Math and English. My teacher for English was a lot older. She was ready to retire. She seemed burnt out. She was sarcastic and flippant. She felt that I should already know the content. She seemed to have an "old school" approach to education that did not fit the current age. It also did not work for me.

The teacher's aid was younger, but not encouraging as all. She often agreed with the main teacher as if they were ganging up on the students. I was not the only one who felt the ridicule. The homework was old fashioned, straight to the point. That was my math teacher, combination special education. Another teacher was, English, was more laid back.

Ridicule

They both said the same thing as the assistant from 4th and 5th grade. It was mostly the teachers that said negative things and make discouraging comments. I felt a sense of shock and humiliation often. I had to read out loud when I did not want to. My sarcastic Math teacher would read grades out in front of class until she was cursed by one of the parents. The students never made fun of me on their own. But the teachers were critical and constantly compared me to other students. They created an environment where I was laughed at as the butt of their jokes.

As an adult, I know that a person can be genuine, direct, and hold you to a standard without being opinionated, judgmental, and sarcastic. Ridicule does not need to be a part of the interaction. The main teacher and the teacher's aide fed off each other. The students would feed off their sarcasm and joking at the expense of other students.

I was happy to see the main teacher retire. I wondered who the new teacher for the new year would be. I felt that any teacher would be better than her. She maintained an uneasy classroom. I was relieved to arrive in class any day and see a different teacher—even a substitute.

I would get made fun of by kids for being a geek. I still held the frustration of elementary school, but I did not act out as much. On top of the learning challenges, was going through puberty and experiencing awkwardness. I brought over a box with my pencils and pens from elementary school. The teacher and teacher's aide made fun of me for having the box on my desk. "That's weird. That's for little kids."

I remember one kid that could read in the class that helped me. He is not doing well today. I thought having a disability would keep me from college, but it did not. I probably could have had a master's degree if I was savvy with the process. My reaction to those classmates was that they would do more than me. They were better in school than me. I looked at them as smarter based on the seed that my grandfather placed within me. I would compare myself to them. But, as adults, they have not achieved what I have achieved. No of them that I see from time to time are doing well.

I told my mother, and she wrote a letter to the teacher. The teacher would react to the letter in class. She would make fun to the point where I would write on small pieces of paper how much I disliked her. She found many of these notes and would make fun of these as well during class time.

I did not have trouble with any of the other teachers in the regular class. All the students treated me the same. I received no grief about how I was learning or what my challenges were. I remember even being asked to read aloud and completed the task with support to sound out words and work through my challenges. No giggling, sarcastic comments, or ridicule was added. I faced my fears in those mainstream classes. Though I still had difficulty reading, I was never made to feel less than. The whole class would say "Hi, Matthew." And "Bye, Matthew." I did not know until later that they were prompted by the teachers to be nice to us. They never treated us poorly, but they may have felt bad for us.

Support from the Teacher

The next year, 8th grade, the replacement teacher truly cared. Her name was Miss Uline. She was more nurturing to the students. She organized lessons more clearly. She made school more fun. The pressure was gone. Gone was the humiliation. She was more prone to explain lessons and clear up student confusion. She would often be at odds with the teacher's aide who maintained her rough approach. It was funny to watch the uptight and uncomfortable process of adaptation that the teacher's aide had to endure. I heard her say aloud a couple of times that she did not approve of the new teacher's methods.

The teacher's aid was not able to run the class. She was forced to conform to what the main teacher organized. The difference was obvious from students to the interactions to the learning. The difference was night and day. She became a better resource even though she was resistant. The power of the main teacher and the ability of a leader to set a tone was demonstrated to me in scores.

I still did not have the support at home. Though it was not as violent and contentious as it once was. My mother began to travel instead of working so much. I was more autonomous. She did not hit me anymore, though I did not rush to sit by her side and read. She was a bit more laid back having connected with a boyfriend about that time.

My defenses came down in the classroom. I no longer felt judged and put on the spot. My confidence grew. I was able to move through the work faster because I was not under pressure. I was able to give my feedback to the teacher and let her know what I thought would help me. I realized that my previous year not being able to provide my feedback left me feeling punished. The classroom held the same standards, but it seemed easier. She gave more homework, but even that did not make the class less enjoyable. The lessons made more sense to me. If they did not, I was not ridiculed for asking questions. The environment was simply well organized.

A Better Way for Students

The replacement teacher seemed to have a better outlook on the students. She was a good teacher. She was hard on me. She pushed. She had a learning disability herself. She was extremely patient and never compared me to other students.

I am a firm believer that this be the requirement for teachers in special education. They must have the ability to empathize with the students and what they are going through.

I learn in action. Even though I stumble, I correct and improve over time. That's the way I would teach someone. That is the approach, but I would also leave out any criticism that sounds like "I told you so," or "You should know this by now." I would give the time for people to learn and grow in their knowledge and practice. Telling someone how to do it does not mean that they picked it up or comprehended enough to put it into action.

When someone tells me that they told me something already, they are being critical. They are trying to prove a point. It feels like an attitude or throwing their weight around. It feels like a punishment more than a learning experience.

Section II: Secondary Education

Chapter 5: Friends

The Summer before high school included a summer youth program. The school district set the program up for special education and low-income students. I enjoyed that program immensely. I made money from my work. It was my money and not my parent's money. My mother helped me open my first bank account. I remembered my grandmother's wisdom to save money and consider what I would do with money before I spent. That beginning savings ended up being the down payment for my first car.

I learned how to fill out a timecard and other employability skills. I learned responsibility. I kept all the documents from the experience. It was the Private Industry Council (PIC) from Saloma County. Though my mom did not want me to work in public works or be a janitor, she was excited to sign me up and have me participate. The students had to be in certain classes or low-income to participate.

Value of Friendship

Making more friends made a difference. Of course, high school was about the image. Junior high had some of that pressure, but I was more innocent and oblivious. In high school, I noticed that attention was given to clothing, what your parents did for work, and where you lived.

I worked in a work-ability program organized through my high school. I worked at Albertson's on Peabody, which is not there anymore. My skills from my first experience transferred well. I learned more about money management from my mom's partner who was an accountant. He taught me about equity and how to run a business. I did not want to be like him, but I wanted to have a similar level of status as an adult. I was keenly aware of the difference between my 20s and his 40 years. He set an example of entrepreneurship and managing a business.

The older I get, the fewer friends we have. I was much more of a loner back in high school. I had about 5 good friends that were more or less connected. I hung out more with the other special education students. We could relate in the experience we were going through. I had "hi and bye" friends from other classes, but more of a connection with the other special ed kids. We were always in the same classes together, so it made sense to hang with them outside of class.

Her name was Ellie. I went out with her for a long time. It was not really serious. She lived fairly far away in Winters, California. I did not know until later, but she was in special education herself. From 9th grade until 11th grade, we were a couple. Back then, I was not sure of myself. I was exploring. I lived internally attempting to figure out the external relationships. I was focused more on the schooling to overcome my challenges.

I learned from my then girlfriend who would overspend on credit cards. My grandparents had already taught me how to save money. Most of my closer friends from high school got comfortable with where they are socially, some on SSI, and giving in to self-limiting. My grandmother began to show signs of dementia.

My frustration was more in 11th grade. My mom put me in tutoring courses, but I could not comprehend the math. I also began attending church. My mom's family was not into church. My grandmother was a southern woman, but never adopted the church life. My father's side was different. Many of them are into church. I wanted to see what it was like.

During one bible study, a bible worker in the church would hear me read. I would stumble over words and not comprehend. The bible worker would turn to me and say, "Oh! He's slow!" The other kids would chuckle.

My grandmother would get frustrated and do the homework for me. She died in 2007 two days after my mother's boyfriend.

I entered a depression. I gained weight. We would have potlucks and I would go back for seconds. That same bible worker would comment under her breath, "Greedy!" I wish I would have engaged her and confronted her more. I believe I would have been happier. When the lady spoke ill of me in her own frustration, I wish I would have been able to educate her. My nervousness in the context of other people I did not know well, my challenges in reading, and that trigger that felt like my mom's frustration limited me. I am no longer interested in attending church.

One of the girls in that Sunday school class is a colleague on my campus. She acts as if she does not know me. I can't wait to show her this book. My expression has evolved. My ability has improved. Self-expression comes naturally for me now. In my early 20s, I read a great deal about communication and self-improvement. They helped tremendously. I have learned to let people know that I just need more time. I am able to redirect them to be more empathetic. I communicate my process of writing it down, practicing, and articulating it aloud. Most people are responsive. I also give myself grace and accept the frustrations of others as normal and their issue not mine. I can see their frustration, but I do not put their pressure on myself.

Self-Expression

Once I was 18, things changed. I was able to get out more and become more of an adult. I straightened myself up from the frustrations that were present in my earlier years.

I was able to express myself. Maybe I could speak for myself and be heard. The only requirement was that people were patient and interested in listening. Rather than feel bad about me, the goal: Find people who are interested in listening.

A lot of my friends from high school were working two jobs and going to college. I did not want to go to college. I definitely did not want a university. I did not want to take out a huge loan to pay for college if I was not going to comprehend. I knew that learning was a challenge. I did not want to fail and have a great amount of debt.

I attended a Junior college. My mother told me that I could live with her if I attended school. I found that they had a large, active disability department. Looking around, I saw people with physical and learning disabilities. I learned to be grateful for my position and ability. That gratitude combined with my mother's advice to never allow them to see me fail.

English and Math were still a challenge. I took each of them 3 times. The fourth time, I would have needed approval to move forward. I received word that the faculty in both cases came together and voted to move me to the next level. I was still stuck.

Trade School

I had a counselor, Arlene, who suggested that I attend trade school because I was taking too long. I felt a slap, but I knew it was true. I needed something that would move me forward. I had been there almost 5 years in junior college. I needed someone to tell me how to progress. My mother was just happy that I was attending college.

Arlene told me to apply to the 6-month course. I chose between medical assistant or administrator. I was able to apply because of my learning disability. I was automatically promoted into the program. I chose administrative assistant training.

My counselor in the program took an attitude toward me because I still lived at home. She seemed thrown off that I was in that position. She must have had experience with others who were slackers symbolized by their living at home with their parents.

Some of my coworkers when I was hired remember me as the person hired from the ROP program. It used to bother me that they called me out. "Oh, I remember when you were ROP." It is like they are pointing out that I am from special education or have a learning disability. It used to bother me. Now, I simply accept this ability as part of my story. I feel better about myself now that I have focused on things that I am really good at. I enjoy teaching others—people with university degrees—about the things I know how to do well.

Chapter 6: IEP

I remember the meetings and the services that were popular for children in my position. I did not realize the example when I was a child. Then again, I wasn't. My mother mentioned that she had a tutor in college. She and he became boyfriend and girlfriend due to the tutoring interaction. She mentioned that she had some challenges with learning. She went back to school when I was in my teens and often talked about rereading things repeatedly. She wanted to get her bachelor's degree, but never finished. She did not struggle per se. She did not announce a disability, but she seemed to study in the same way I did.

My grandfather must have had a disability that he never announced. He remained a janitor all his life. He was a veteran of World War II. My grandmother would always question why he would not get a better job with benefits. He was born in a time when you could get a stable job without college. I feel he would have gone beyond 6th grade education if it was something he was good at. He would call me stupid when I was a child. When I got older, I would return the insult. It was our way of familial banter. It was not malicious even though it was landed when I was mad at him. Beyond his janitorial work, he bought properties including some in Vina, CA. He rented the property out to a doctor who kept an orchard in Haight-Ashbury neighborhood of San Francisco, California in the 1960s. I remember the doctor who rented the home and the orchard from my grandparents. They eventually sold it to him. They lived well in retirement from that sale.

Their house in San Francisco where they raised my mother and her siblings set the standard for me of legacy and real estate. It demonstrated how a family builds real wealth. It also demonstrates the gentrification and missed opportunities of financial wealth. My mother was against selling the San Francisco family home. It was sold during the Great Recession. My uncles and aunts share her regret now that the property value has exploded. The advice that stuck with me was to always save money. Every time I get a bonus from my job, I use it for investments. I look for opportunities.

My mother would always discourage me from washing toilets for work. She was always about education, but she only taught me what she knew. She learned more from her boyfriend who was an accountant. My mother paid for a tutor for math due to my struggles in high school. I did not absorb a lot of it, but the lesson I learned was about accepting help. When I decided to go back to school in my late twenties, I was open to connecting with tutors and accepting that I could get help.

My Father

My father was a visitor. He would always bring me books. My mom and dad seemed to have an unspoken agreement. They did not get along when I was younger. Dad was concerned about child support and being present for me. My father taught me how to repair vehicles and other technical repairs. My father would sit with me and study spelling bee words or homework sometimes. He brought educational games over and other help like quiz cards. He would visit sometimes, spend the night, and watch movies with me. I would never visit his side of the family. This was the rule until I was about 14.

My father was in denial about my disability. He was a mechanic early in my life. He became an operational engineer later in life. He never discouraged me, but he never encouraged either. He set an example by receiving an associate degree. He also attended and completed trade school. He did not face a disability or announce it though he mentioned that others in the family had learning disabilities. I think he went into a career that he was good at. He thrived because the bar was set to a level he could crush.

I discovered my talent in the middle of my life and career. I was better at money management than my parents. They stressed education and college, but I found that college was not for me. My mother's partner of 10 years passed away from cancer. Before he died, he taught me about equity and the lifestyle I wanted to live. He had a nice car, bought new. He owned property that he had sold by the time he met my mother. He taught me about real estate. His parents said something that stuck with me, "Never take more money in credit than you have in the bank to pay it back."

Interestingly, after I purchased my first place, my mother & father started their friendship over again. They reconnected and would hang out, even taking trips together. After the pressures of raising a child, they seemed to find a calm between the two of them.

Education & Services

My mom attended Individualized Education Program (IEP) meetings. I remember switching schools because the teachers were not allowing me to advance. Special education is one option. Resource education is the higher option. The teachers would not allow me to pursue the challenge of resource education. My IEP scores were not high enough. Ninth and tenth grade felt repetitive. The classes were combination classes. It felt like I was not advancing with the lessons. It seemed like the special education classes were not giving us serious work.

The school offered me the opportunity to take an IQ test around this time. I was not forced to take it. I wanted to. I scored a few points lower than I should to be considered average. I felt that the limiter was the classes that I was enrolled in. I needed more of a challenge in my mind. I was discouraged thinking that I would never grow out of my learning difficulties. Math was my only true difficulty. I was also low in English due to reading difficulties.

The pressure was gone in my interactions with my mom. She seemed less intense and more lenient as she had a boyfriend that supported her. She gave me more choices rather than ultimatums. It was up to me to finish school on time and engage with the content. She supported me with tutors and other assistance.

My mom signed the transfer to Vacaville Highschool to Will Wood school for high school. My grandmother entered dementia during that time which increased my stress. She was almost like my mother, so it was tough. I persevered.

I did okay in school after home school studies. I wanted to experience senior-class social activities like prom and other activities. I met new friends and enjoyed that year. The more I studied, the better I got it seemed. In other scholastic tests, I scored in the average range with no obvious deficiencies. When it came to a description, I would say I was a decent student. I took Summer School to catch up on things that I missed and graduated with honors even as a special education student. I guess I did alright.

A child needs someone to explain and walk them through the challenges knowing that the solution is not to attempt to be "normal" but to work through to create a "different" way to achieve. In addition to the reduction of pressure my mom grew into, she talked to me with less aggression and scolding. She would talk about the alternatives and the outcomes of my choices. My rebellion was a reaction to her aggression. Discipline with children must include patience, choice presentation, and outcome explanations. Make it about outcomes that come with support, not consequences that come with a threat. Rather than talking about what will be taken away or help that will cease, speak more about the structure and opportunities that can be gained from high achievement and personal responsibility.

I am convinced that parents scold their children too much. When a child has a learning challenge, they internalize the aggression rather than any of the lessons. Once my mother began to talk to me with calm and expectation of better outcomes, my response improved. I thought about my dreams and aspirations rather than the scolding. I could see how my choices could get me to my goals even while the lessons in school were challenging. I could persevere even when I was not perfect. I see more parents in my observations today speaking and explaining to children. I see fewer slaps and violence than I did growing up. I know that this works better.

Chapter 7: Caught Up

Wanting to Be Caught with my class was a pressure. But I was not ready. I left my options open to see what I was good at. I came to the realization that I was not prepared. I needed more time and attention.

Prom Memories

Time was a tremendous importance in my life. I always looked at things as taking advantage of the time. I went to three proms. I went to prom with my girlfriend when I was 16. She was 2 years older than me. I attended my prom with a friend. I also went to prom with my friend who was a year younger than me. I just wanted to maximize the time.

Prom attendance required good grades. You could not attend the prom if you did not have good grades. The prom was an achievement for me. It was not the level of a graduation, but it was a reward for staying current. My father never went to prom. My mother never attended either. My father worked to receive his GED and eventually an associate degree, but he did not enjoy the experience of prom. In this way, prom was an opportunity as well as a reward. The pictures, the dancing, the food, and the fun were things I will never forget. It reflected my experiences as a child. I reminisced about all those movies that I grew up watching. Pretty in Pink, St. Elmo's Fire, Breakfast Club, and the television shows I grew up with created a mystique around the prom.

The other thing about prom was that it was a great equalizer. Every student was in the same place and no different from the others. We had all kept up with our grades. We had all achieved this milestone. I remember working and saving up for the prom. It was a lesson in independence and the reward of saving.

Choice to Something Different

I remember taking an economics class in high school. I recognized an acumen for money and economics. I remember my mom paid for some of the first prom, but I paid for the other two. Economics did not seem as complicated as Math. Formulas were present, but they seemed simple. The teacher was not a special education teacher, but the lessons seemed common sense to me. I dealt with those concepts while working and engaging with saving, making payments, and affording the things I wanted. I was able to get an idea about balancing checkbooks and writing checks, but financial terms and reasoning were also vital to me. The procedures and policies seemed to click for me. This was real life.

Some others of my special education group seemed to catch on as well. The pressure was released. I knew the answers when the teacher would call on me. I was able to manage the real-life situations that were presented to me. Others seemed to excel as well. It was an integrated classroom with mainstream students and special education students. The teacher was laid back, but on top of the lessons. It was a course that I wished every student could have though other schools did not have the course.

I began to develop an interest in accounting in high school. I also noticed that my mother's partner was an accountant. I liked that idea. I dwelled on my disability too much as a child. As I became an adult, I was caught comparing myself to others. I was more aware of it as a reality, but it became a challenge. I would bring this up to her partner, and he would confirm that I was not competent. He based it on the fact that I was in the disabled student program. I hate that word now. "Competent." He said that a few times. It was difficult because I looked up to him. I knew that I wanted to do something different from the norm. I was not made for the academic process. That narrative was serviceable for a while, but thankfully, I shook that later.

Real World Learning

My grandparents raised me most of the time even though my mother was present. They would compare me with my older cousin. She has a master's degree, but now wants to do real estate like me.

My mom hurt herself in 2005. She injured her rotator cuff as a nurse MTA. She was placed on leave. She was forced to retire once the leave ran out. I was just finishing my ROP program. I was making my own money while living in her home. She told me, "Matthew, I am no longer working. I have no income. You need to pay the mortgage here." I was shocked. It was like a fire under my butt though. I love my mom and wanted to support her financially. I questioned whether I could.

Her partner's experience with his business was not well. He lost a business relationship with his father. His income diminished. His business went down. He eventually battled cancer, removing his income from the household. He died in 2007.

I grew up taking care of my grandparents as they took care of me. By this time, my grandfather was deceased, and my grandmother was in a nursing home. I had the confidence and understanding to take over my mother's household. The home had to survive off my single, smaller income. This confidence was critical.

In 2006, I began working at my new job. I began to kick in and pay the bills. I was living with them. Neither of them was able to pay.

Her partner began to reverse his words about me. He never apologized for how he talked to me prior to this, but I knew I was different in his mind. It was a difference that I never thought I would see. My mother always told me not to allow others to talk me into a lesser view of myself. Her partner predicted my failure. He was depressed and was not always the most encouraging person.

I knew that I was smarter than I thought. I was taking care of a household of four including my sister. By the time my mother was receiving her retirement income, I had handled the expenses of the household allowing my mother to get back on her feet. When I purchased my own home, she was offended, but no one could downplay my progress or take away from my confidence.

Section III: Higher Learning

Chapter 8: Discovery

2001-2005 Junior College, Regional Occupational Program (ROP) completed 2006. They had great connections with employers including the hospital in Solano County.

I applied to college. I did not want to waste the money and attend college when I knew I was not ready. I also did not want to short myself. I did not want to regret my choice being too safe. I wanted to put myself out there in some way. My reflections on my mother's partner and my grandfather, my grandmother, my mother, and my father remind me to state that you should never rely only on family for support. You must engage professional help as well. I have benefitted from a counselor as well as the guidance counselors who shaped my education and options.

I talked with a counselor. I spoke up about not feeling normal. My mother never said that I could not do it. I took the responsibility to look for something that would speak to me. Even though I was not the best reader, I read the Power of Positive thinking. I was frustrated and tore the pages because my transformation was not happening fast enough. I willed my confidence to increase. I just maintain progress even if it was simple movement. I searched for options including other self-help books, courses, and worksheets. I remembered how my grandfather would always tell me that I was young. I thought of myself as young and able to change. It was not a plan for self-improvement, but it was a commitment. That is more important.

You don't always need a plan, but you need to focus on learning, self-improvement, and support. I studied with friends. I moved slowly. I gave myself space and grace with a list of goals. I read. I sought counseling, and I engaged the support programs I found in college moving forward. Give yourself time even if it takes more time. Give yourself credit even if it is a slow achievement. Know that your feelings will be hurt. But also know that an open mind will find new resources that support advancement.

My focus was to stay in school. I wanted to stay in a learning environment but did not want the pressures of a university. I accepted the fact that I needed more help. I did not look at it as a disadvantage because of my college orientation. I knew there were options and support available to me.

I wanted to make sure that I tried. That way, I would have no regrets. I applied to a couple of 4-year colleges though I was set on attending junior college as a steppingstone to the bigger schools. I saw the pattern of other students finding their way as they entered college. I knew I wanted to be a white-collar worker though my family was more blue collar. I could not pinpoint my talent at an early age. I knew my potential was blue collar, but I wanted something different.

I remained open through testing and assessments like the Myers-Briggs test. I scored high in finance and management. No matter what others told me, I stayed optimistic about what I could do even outside of my comfort zone. I looked at it as good risk and bad risks. Good risks include the risk of time when you are young to apply yourself and figure out what works for you and what you are good at.

English in Multiple Tries

My aunt that had special needs passed away in 2002, a year after I started junior college. That was harder on me. She was only 36. It hurt more than my grandparents. She was the one who taught me manners. She was developmentally delayed and stuck in one spot. I did not want to be like her. She encouraged me to do better.

College was a challenge in general, but the loss of my aunt made it harder. It felt good to have the control of college that was different from high school. It was nice to be integrated with other "normal" students and older people. I noticed people with greater learning disabilities. The teachers were accommodating. The support department was large and followed up. I would meet up with friends in the library after classes and feel supported. I had more people to reach out to that I trusted.

Some may think that it is embarrassing to attend and seek help from the resource center. It is different from high school. The stigma is not there. The older people there made me realize that I was not as behind as I thought. They were in their 30s and 40s figuring it out and attending college. I thought I was the only one behind but seeing them told me that I was doing okay. I learned to put less pressure on myself. The goal to finish is appropriate, but I did not want to be too hard on myself.

It is never too late to fulfill your dream of learning and employment and the life you desire. I was relieved that I had time. The decision toward junior college was a good one.

English and Math continued to be my tough subjects. I took the same courses multiple times with different teachers. I felt like I had to start all over again each time I got a new teacher. They have a curriculum to follow, but the differences in personality, grading, and support were so varied that I could not figure it out. I remember one teacher would have one opinion about my writing. I would make all the corrections in the writing lab. Returning to the teacher was frustrating. The teachers and the writing lab instructors were not on the same page. Even though the lessons were the same, the specificity and detail among them was too different for me.

I knew I was failing and signed up with the department chair to get approval to take it again. I remember getting a pass once the department noticed that I was taking it multiple times.

Confidence not Competence

I met a group with learning disabilities for support. We talked about disability sometimes, but more than that, we identified and related to one another. I remain friends with them.

After you hit a certain age, confidence takes over the path toward your success. I took the same courses in another college and passed them with no problem. Something clicked for me. I felt I was younger, too young and did not have the life experiences to go along with the lessons.

It is a lesson that I have learned in the context of my learning ability. I am all about practical applications. If I can relate to the lesson, I can comprehend and replicate the skill. Without that, I look like I don't know what I'm doing. Application is critical. Real-life situations are key. You may not have real-life experiences but get good at making them up. I remember in math; I would skip the equations and move to the word problems that I could understand in application. Even if you must add something to or substitute, focus on learning the process. Check with the teacher and encourage them to make the question plain to you in the context of your example.

That's exactly what I did at my job. The list of tasks and procedures was long. I had trouble listening to the training. The learning was not fully clicking. I learned more from my coworker coming over and critiquing me in the moment while patients were in front of me.

I have achieved more of course. I know I can handle college better if I was to attend now. More than just the college curriculum, I have a proven ability to handle real life and survive paying bills, making purchases, and excelling in my career. My mom never underestimated me, but her partner did. My ability showed him that I could not only be a responsible adult, but I could take care of other adults.

My greatest confidence came from the purchase of my first home. I purchased my first house and obtained a decent job. I found that competence is not within any academic pursuit but within the passion you have and your ability to create a life for yourself that you can be happy with.

Though I am confident that I can go back to college, I know I can make more money continuing in real estate. I would like to take courses on topics that I am interested in rather than working toward a degree. I began with a hobby working with real estate. More than the college for a job, I am thinking about practical life, real estate to support the lifestyle I want which may include some college courses for fun.

Chapter 9: Quality of Life

During the time my mother would slap me, she was going through a divorce that she filed for. She was stressed. They split up for 10 years. Like 1985 or 1986 when I was 4 or 5 years old. In 1993, mom had saved enough money to execute the divorce. She and my father did not get along. My dad has told me that he entertained multiple women.

Once she purchases a home and met a new partner in 1994, she lost some of the pressure. She was a happier person. He positively influenced my mom. He was more academic. He seemed to present her with ideas. He was an accountant and was more structured. We had dinners at the table or ate at restaurants. We went to different places and enjoyed a higher experience of travel. Her partner would educate us on different sites and the richness of the state of California. He always researched the history and culture of the places we visited. He was a tour guide of sorts. My mom was tight-lipped about her feelings, but I noticed her cuddles and kissing as shows of affection. She was obviously in a better space with him.

Mom Passing Away

In 2014 My mom passed away. She had a good pension, but she was spending beyond her means. I noticed that she was becoming a bit slower, forgetful, and sluggish. I went back home often and worked to help her even while owning my own property. She was not moving as well as she had before. She began to drop things. I helped her pay her bills with her money. I was able to fix things around her house, balance her checkbook, and get her spending under control.

March of 2013, my mom began coughing and exhibiting slurred speech. They thought she had a stroke. The stroke evaluation came back negative. The ER referred her to a neurologist. The neurologist diagnosed her with Bulbar ALS. It affected her esophagus and upper torso. She was not able to swallow as her throat lost its ability to operate. The disease progressed and she needed a feeding tube. She was unable to hold her saliva. She aged incredibly fast at that point. Her nutrition was depleted. Her saliva began to require suction, or it would fill her lungs. She would need to live in a nursing home to be suctioned continually.

She decided to pass away naturally. I wanted her to pass away at home rather than at a hospital. I took care of her during those 4-6 months while she declined. We employed a hospice agency. I saw too many people who raised me pass away in the hospital. My grandmother. My grandfather. I was not willing to see her in a hospital. I gained my closure and had my chance to see my mother work through her final days on her own terms.

Confidence Gain

Managing my mom's household added to the confidence I had in my own ability to create a life for myself. I began to thrive. I told myself that she made her decisions and chose her end. I kept in mind that she lived for herself. I remember her crying and telling me of her pride in my sister and me. She wrote it. She was unable to speak at the time.

I prepared my mom's things after she was gone. I went to counseling for grieving and attended support groups. I kept family heirlooms and dispensed with things I knew my mom would not care about. I had to become strong in ways that I had not experienced before. My mom and her siblings were not as close as they were when my grandparents were alive. They attended her funeral, but I was not dependent upon them for support or direction after my parent was gone. They never told me that they were proud, but I could see that they respected me. That alone gave me confidence as I took care of the emotional tasks that I alone had to take. My sister was not interested in working through the specifics. I shared what my mother would want shared and put away the heirlooms.

I remembered a book called positive thinking. "Turn a negative into a positive." I put the money she left into use to update her home for renting it. The revenue from that rental is shared with my sister to this day.

Moving While Grieving

I purchased a duplex, painted it by hand, and got it ready to rent. I kept moving physically even while I was grieving. I worked long nights in physical labor to keep from feeling the pain of the loss and the anger from not having help.

I began buying properties and establishing multiple streams of revenue. This is important because the regular job, your employment, is not yours. You serve at the pleasure of your employer. Real estate businesses are great for tax write offs, passive income, and becoming the employer. Your tax situation changes drastically reducing your liability. Your income is not dependent only upon your employer. You gain the ability to direct others in service to your properties.

I came up with my own thing and began to think about doing things differently. I moved into a trade school at the suggestion of a college counselor. I was introduced to real estate through a friend.

My creation of my own lane happened slowly. It is starting to add up. I call it "halfway to retirement." I have reduced my workload to 20 hours just to keep my health benefits.

I feel like the people who were higher achievers in high school attempted to do what others had done. They failed because the path that others took did not work for them. Their confidence was lost, and they eventually fell, relying on the system for their support. They fell into the safety net of society rather than excelling in their own lane.

Finding my Niche in Real Estate Entrepreneurship

It's just basic math. Bookkeeping is computerized and allows me to keep up. My mentor helped. In 2008, I bought my first property. I invested $3000 worth of repairs in a property that was not my own so that it would pass FHA. It worked out. I have been in the real estate business since 2008 and now own 4 properties.

To me, residual income means that I can work less and still have the same lifestyle. When you build your business to the point where it's completely passive, that's when you'll have true freedom. This is a goal I did not know was important until it became possible for me.

Knowing and accepting your worth is an important part of being successful as an entrepreneur; otherwise, there's little chance that other people will take notice or pay attention when the time comes for them to consider working with or buying from someone like yourself.

You're going to start by learning some new skills, which will help you build an income. Then you'll use that income to increase your skills, so that you can make more money. And then you'll continue increasing the amount of money that comes into your life while learning more and more about the world around us.

Ownership

Pride in self is a sign of self-confidence, which is an essential component of success. Pride in yourself is also important because it allows you to be honest with yourself and others. If you have no pride, you'll lose respect for your work and yourself, which can lead to failure. Even if you work hard but are not proud of what you do, no one else will be either.

Owning property feels like freedom. It is also extremely rewarding. You have pride in the property and the people who live there are lucky to have you as their landlord. Know that you will never be bored again because you will always have something to work on!

All I had to do was learn new skills and build upon them. The skills were a new focus on what I enjoyed and was good at rather than attempting something that did not fit for me.

In the end, all I had to do was stop beating myself up for the things that I could not do well. Learn new skills and build upon them. The skills were a new focus on what I enjoyed and was good at rather than attempting something that did not fit for me. It's critical to remember that we are our own best advocates and there is no one else who will be as passionate about our success as ourselves.

60   This Ability

The most important thing is to find your niche. Know that it will be work, but it will be delightful work. I found my niche and the sky is the limit!

Chapter 10: Finally Moving Out

I moved from my mother's house long ago. I still had to move into my own. Moving out of other people's ability to judge me is the goal. That is my challenge to overcome. The job for the others—the helpers, the counselors, the bible workers, and all the other adults—is to address the facts of each situation with opportunities for growth and progress. Help individuals to locate the opportunities. Let them do what they can do for themselves, dare them to. The result will initially feel like a slap in the face, but the autonomy gained from rising to the challenge and do it for themselves is invaluable.

I do the same thing in my day job. I never tell people simply, "You're late!" I have learned to offer solutions even in the reality of their lateness. "You're late. I can see what the doctor says and offer a rescheduled time that works for you." I find that most people respond well to this approach of solutions even in the face of the challenge.

I have listened to colleagues who want me to be more cut and dry. They think I have trouble saying no when a no is warranted.

They want me to follow their way of doing it. I come from emergency room experiences where no gets things thrown at you. I offer a more nuanced approach. "No. We can't do that, but I can see what other options we have available." I diffuse situations with that approach rather than needing to call security with every patient that does not get their way.

Paying it Forward

I remember remodeling a friend's house. She was a social worker for the nursing department on my unit and partially blind. She kind of reminded me of my mom in a way. Her attitude and some of her ways appealed to me. She had kids that were my age. They were motivated, but did not help in the way that I would. They were not into remodeling. They were good at what they did, but I wanted to do something nice for someone.

It was also a repayment for the talks that we had during work hours. She was a benefit to me. I felt great to help someone just like I was helping my mother when she was alive. It did my heart good to improve someone's quality of life.

I remember her daughter gave me some resistance in the beginning, but she warmed up as she saw me doing some work. I changed fixtures, made repairs, painted, installed floors, and other things within her house. She was always a help to people in her community.

As much as I enjoyed the process and the giving back, I learned that I need to focus on myself and ensure that I am not just giving my all to others. I must take care of my own health and well-being. If not, I could wear myself out. Even helping must be balanced.

Building my Empire

I diversified my portfolio to the point where I could live off the income from the investments. I am almost at the point where I meet my monthly income from work through my investments. I have the financial freedom to lower my hours at my traditional job.

I would like to expand my real estate investing to the point where I can focus on it full-time. I want to retire early from the employment world.

Take the risks. Don't be reckless but take the initiative to find out what you do not know. Talk to thought leaders and researchers. Focus on the advice of people who have been through the experience. Take the lead of people who have been where you want to be. Refuse to listen to people who are loud and think they know. Whether it's money, school, investments, career, or hobby, find what feels like it is not work. Enjoy each of the ways you make money.

I enjoy working with my hands. Hands on real estate is perfect for me. I enjoy the money activities as well like bitcoin or dogecoin. I am not on the side of instant gratification. Delayed gratification is more certain. Consider how your desired future will be supported by the activities that you are taking now. It is the risk that helps you get ahead, but not for quick gains and getting rich quickly. Plan for the long haul.

Finding My Happiness

I have friends who went through the same classes but have not decided to move forward. Their happiness suffers. I know one who drinks excessively. He could read better, but that did not translate into opportunities for them. He built up a crutch rather than giving up.

I remember a colleague who wanted me to fax using the feeder rather than opening and laying the document on the scanner. She was adamant that the feeder was the best way to process the paperwork. I have experience with some crappy machines in the past. They would often clog and present other problems due to problems with the document feeder. If I only have one or two pages, I have learned that it is just as much effort to open, place, scan, and send as it is to fumble with a clogged scanner. I scanned my way, and my colleague seemed genuinely surprised that it worked. "See," I said. "I just did it another way, but the result was the same." She nodded with acceptance.

You can achieve sustainable happiness doing it your way. This ability is one that everyone should come to know and implement daily. Do not ever feel like someone owes you something. Always focus on your responsibility and how you will execute alone even when others are contracted to help. Have back up plans and options. Make sure you know what your happiness is and how to achieve it your way.

Matthew T. Sampson
Author Bio of Resilience

I'm Matthew T. Sampson of Resilience, age 40, I was a "bright-eyed and bushy-tailed" kid in special Ed with resilience, now I'm looking to help parents see how my learning deficit on how it effects a kid subconsciously through my story, how a kid can overcome with using his or her talent into a successful career as an adult. I was the kid that rode in the short yellow bus. I knew I was different by riding that bus. The rides were fun though. My parents supported me, but they did not completely understand how my learning deficit affected me psychologically. I did not have the ability to explain it either. I could not read in fourth grade. I struggled in the Vacaville system of special education from 1989 all the way through the 1990s, until I graduated in the 2001. I dealt with deficits in reading, writing, and comprehension through graduation and into college. I'm a strong believer in education to a certain degree, no matter if it's in college, trade school, or self-education. True learning is all about taking the initiative to develop your talents in what your good at.

As an adult in my late 30s when writing, I'm excited. At age 40, I have taken the opportunity to write this book. I present it from the hope to help someone who is in a similar situation as me. I want to relieve the pressure and overwhelm. I want you to know that you are not the only one who feels the stress. You can choose any number of possible ways to be successful. Regardless of your formal training or educational achievement, you can use your talent and experience gained from adulting to excel in a career.

I learned how to cope with my learning deficit. As important, I leaned into my interests. When I discovered my gift, I was freed. My talent led into confidence. My confidence became stronger when assisting my parents when times got tough in their finances and their health. My interests and experiences led me into entrepreneurship as a way of not only surviving but thriving with good money management, home improvement DIY skills, success in real estate investing, and running an online store. That led me into financial freedom. I'm thankful to have an opportunity to also share my strategy of initiative and persistence following my talent to become my best.

Made in the USA
Monee, IL
27 June 2023

37736854R00039